Breakfast & Brunch

- Introduction — 2
- Pancakes & Waffles — 4
- Economical Eggs — 24
- Muffins & More — 42
- Hot & Hearty — 62
- Index — 80

Eating Well. Spending Less.

Budgeting has become a national pastime these days. Cooking more meals at home and shopping smarter are two huge steps in the right direction. Add the recipes in this book and your family will actually eat better while you save money.

DOING THE MATH

Every recipe in this collection was individually priced to determine the cost per serving. Keep in mind that food costs vary regionally and seasonally, so exact prices per serving are not included. For budget planning, each recipe is marked with either the 99¢ or Less icon or the Budget Friendly icon next to the recipe title.

 Per serving, this recipe does not cost more than 99¢ to make.

 Per serving, this recipe does not cost more than $1.99 to make.

- All calculations are based on actual grocery store prices. The least expensive ingredients available were chosen, including some store-brand products and sale items.

- Prices include all ingredients as listed in the recipe, except salt, pepper and ingredients labeled as "optional."

- If a range is offered for the amount of an ingredient (1/8 teaspoon to 1/4 teaspoon, for example), the smaller amount was used to calculate the cost per serving.

- If an ingredient is presented with an option (3/4 cup chopped tomatoes or red bell peppers, for example), the first item listed was used to calculate the cost per serving.

- If there is a range of serving sizes (makes 4 to 6 servings, for example), the larger number of servings was used to calculate the cost per serving.

- Food shown in the photo that is not listed as an ingredient (including garnishes, optional items and serving suggestions) was not included in the cost per serving.

Hungry for Money-Saving Tips?

Plan Ahead.

Think about the meals you need to make and write a shopping list. Then check the cupboards, fridge and freezer to see what you have on hand. It's all too easy to buy another jar of something that's already sitting on the shelf. Check sale flyers while you're planning and keep an open mind. If there's an amazing price on eggs or bacon, you may want to plan on having breakfast for dinner, too. Don't forget the coupons and never shop hungry.

Resist Temptation.

Grocery stores are in the business of getting you to buy things. You can literally trip over brightly colored stacks of products in the aisles—tempting, but not necessarily economical. Before you head down an aisle, check the overhead sign that tells you what you'll find there. Save time by skipping the entire aisle if it doesn't have anything you need.

When is a Bargain Not a Bargain?

A super sale on cottage cheese is no bargain if you won't use it up before the expiration date. And don't always assume a bigger package is a better buy. You need to do the math or check the labels on the edge of the shelves. Most stores will list a price per ounce for each different size. Don't assume you have to buy four items if the sale sign reads "4 for $4" either. Usually you can purchase only one item and get the same deal.

Waste Not, Want Not.

Pay attention to what kind of food ends up in the garbage at your house. Could you buy less or serve smaller portions? Rethink leftovers. They can make a great packed lunch. You can also freeze individual portions for later. Many breakfast foods, like pancakes and waffles, freeze well and can be reheated in a toaster oven.

Start the Day Right.

Skip breakfast and you risk giving in to an expensive coffee and pastry later. Making breakfast at home is healthier and more economical. Best of all, with the recipes in this book, it's a delicious start to any day.

Pancakes & Waffles

Puffy Pancake

99¢ or Less

- 3 tablespoons melted butter, divided
- ½ cup all-purpose flour
- ½ cup milk
- 2 eggs
- ¼ teaspoon salt
- 2 bananas, sliced
- 1 cup sliced strawberries
- 2 tablespoons chocolate syrup
- Powdered sugar (optional)

1. Preheat oven to 400°F. Pour 2 tablespoons butter into large ovenproof skillet; brush onto side of skillet.

2. Combine flour, milk, eggs, remaining 1 tablespoon butter and salt in medium bowl; whisk constantly 1 minute. Pour batter into prepared skillet.

3. Bake 20 to 22 minutes or until pancake is golden brown and puffs up side of skillet. Remove from oven and immediately fill with fruit. Drizzle with chocolate syrup; sprinkle with powdered sugar, if desired.

Makes 3 to 4 servings

Note: This pancake can also be prepared in a deep-dish pie plate.

Chocolate Cherry Pancakes

99¢ or less

- 2 cups all-purpose flour
- 1 cup dried cherries
- 2/3 cup semisweet chocolate chips
- 1/3 cup sugar
- 4½ teaspoons baking powder
- ½ teaspoon baking soda
- ½ teaspoon salt
- 1½ cups milk
- 2 eggs
- ¼ cup (½ stick) butter, melted
- Pancake syrup (optional)

1. Combine flour, cherries, chocolate chips, sugar, baking powder, baking soda and salt in large bowl; mix well. Beat milk, eggs and butter in medium bowl until well blended.

2. Add milk mixture to flour mixture; stir just until moistened. (Add ¼ to ½ cup additional milk if thinner pancakes are desired.)

3. Heat griddle or large nonstick skillet over medium heat until drop of water sizzles when dropped on surface. For each pancake, spoon ¼ cup batter onto hot griddle. Cook until golden brown on both sides.

Makes 20 to 24 pancakes (6 to 8 servings)

tip: To be even more frugal, substitute dried cranberries, which are a bit cheaper, for the dried cherries. A little dried fruit goes a long way, since the sweetness and flavor are concentrated. Dried fruit keeps for a long time, too, so there's less waste than with fresh fruit. Per pound it can seem expensive, but in use it's often a bargain.

Pancakes & Waffles 7

Oatmeal Pecan Pancakes

1¼ to 1½ cups milk, divided
½ cup old-fashioned oats
⅔ cup all-purpose flour
⅓ cup whole wheat flour
2½ tablespoons packed light brown sugar
2 teaspoons baking powder
½ teaspoon baking soda
¼ teaspoon salt
1 egg
2 tablespoons melted butter
½ cup chopped toasted pecans
Pancake syrup (optional)

1. Bring ½ cup milk to a simmer in small saucepan. Stir in oats. Remove from heat; set aside 10 minutes.

2. Combine flours, brown sugar, baking powder, baking soda and salt in large bowl; mix well.

3. Combine egg and melted butter in small bowl; mix well. Stir in oatmeal mixture and ¾ cup milk. Add egg mixture to dry ingredients; stir just to combine. Do not beat. If mixture is too thick to spoon, add remaining ¼ cup milk, 1 tablespoon at a time. Add pecans; stir just to combine.

4. Lightly butter large skillet or griddle; heat over medium heat. Drop batter by ¼ cupfuls; do not crowd skillet. Flatten batter slightly to form pancakes. Cook about 2 minutes until tops are bubbly. Turn and cook until golden brown. *Makes 4 servings*

 To toast pecans, spread in single layer in heavy-bottomed skillet. Cook over medium heat 1 to 2 minutes, stirring frequently, until nuts are lightly browned. Remove from skillet immediately; cool before using.

Pancakes & Waffles

Devil's Food Pancakes

99¢ or LESS

try other flavors

- 1 package (about 18 ounces) devil's food cake mix
- 2 cups milk
- 2 eggs
- ½ cup mini chocolate chips
- Powdered sugar
- Strawberry Glaze (recipe follows, optional)

1. Whisk cake mix, milk and eggs in large bowl until well blended. Stir in chocolate chips.

2. Heat griddle or large nonstick skillet over medium-low to medium heat. (Do not cook pancakes at a higher temperature as they burn easily.) Pour ¼ cup batter onto griddle for each pancake. Cook 3 to 4 minutes or until edges appear dry; turn and cook 2 to 3 minutes. Repeat with remaining batter.

3. Sprinkle with powdered sugar and serve with Strawberry Glaze.

Makes 4 servings (about 22 pancakes)

Strawberry Glaze: Combine 1 cup chopped fresh strawberries and ⅓ cup strawberry preserves in medium bowl; mix well.

tip | If you have leftovers, it's nice to know that, like most pancakes, these freeze well. Freeze four pancakes in one resealable freezer bag. Reheat in the microwave.

Classic Waffles

2¼ cups all-purpose flour
2 tablespoons sugar
1 tablespoon baking powder
½ teaspoon salt
2 cups milk
2 eggs, beaten
¼ cup vegetable oil

1. Preheat waffle iron according to manufacturer's directions.

2. Sift flour, sugar, baking powder and salt in large bowl. Combine milk, eggs and oil in medium bowl. Stir liquid ingredients into dry ingredients until moistened.

3. For each waffle, pour about ¾ cup batter onto waffle iron. Close lid and cook until steaming stops.* Garnish as desired.

Makes 4 servings

Check the manufacturer's directions for recommended amount of batter and baking time.

Chocolate Waffles: Substitute ¼ cup unsweetened cocoa powder for ¼ cup flour and add ¼ teaspoon vanilla to liquid ingredients. Proceed as directed above.

Tip: For crispier waffles, use less batter and let them cook for a few seconds longer after the steaming has stopped.

Peach Pecan Upside-Down Pancake

2 tablespoons butter, melted
2 tablespoons packed light brown sugar
1 tablespoon pancake syrup
½ (16-ounce) package frozen unsweetened peach slices, thawed
3 tablespoons pecan pieces
⅔ cup biscuit baking mix
2 eggs
⅓ cup milk
½ teaspoon vanilla
Additional pancake syrup (optional)

1. Preheat oven to 400°F. Spray 8- or 9-inch pie pan with nonstick cooking spray.

2. Pour butter into pie pan. Sprinkle with brown sugar and drizzle with pancake syrup. Arrange peach slices in single layer on top in circle. Sprinkle with pecans.

3. Place baking mix in medium bowl. Whisk together eggs, milk and vanilla in small bowl; stir into baking mix just until dry ingredients are moistened. Pour batter over peaches.

4. Bake 15 to 18 minutes or until lightly browned and toothpick inserted into center comes out clean. Cool 1 minute. Run knife around outer edge of pan. Invert pancake onto serving plate. Cut into 6 wedges. Serve immediately with additional syrup, if desired.

Makes 4 to 6 servings

Blueberry Pancakes with Blueberry-Spice Syrup

- 1 cup all-purpose flour
- 2 tablespoons sugar
- 2 teaspoons baking powder
- ¼ teaspoon salt
- ¾ cup milk
- 2 eggs
- 1 tablespoon butter, melted
- ½ cup blueberries
- **Blueberry-Spice Syrup (recipe follows)**
- **Nonstick cooking spray**

1. Combine flour, sugar, baking powder and salt in medium bowl. Beat milk and eggs in small bowl; stir in butter. Add milk mixture to flour mixture, stirring until almost smooth. Gently fold in blueberries.

2. Prepare Blueberry-Spice Syrup; set aside.

3. Coat large nonstick skillet with cooking spray. Heat over medium heat until water droplets sprinkled on skillet bounce off surface. Pour ¼ cup batter onto skillet for each pancake. Cook 2 to 3 minutes or until tops of pancakes are bubbly; turn and cook 2 minutes or until bottoms are lightly browned. Serve with Blueberry-Spice Syrup.

Makes 4 servings

Blueberry-Spice Syrup

- ½ cup blueberries, divided
- ½ cup pancake syrup, divided
- ½ teaspoon grated lemon peel (optional)
- ½ teaspoon ground cinnamon
- ¼ teaspoon ground nutmeg

Bring ¼ cup blueberries and ¼ cup syrup to a boil in small saucepan over medium heat. Mash hot berries with fork. Add remaining ¼ cup blueberries, ¼ cup syrup, lemon peel, if desired, cinnamon and nutmeg. Cook and stir over medium heat about 2 minutes or until heated through.

Makes 1 cup

Pancakes & Waffles 17

Cornmeal Pancakes

- 2 cups buttermilk
- 2 eggs, lightly beaten
- ¼ cup sugar
- 2 tablespoons butter, melted
- 1½ cups yellow cornmeal
- ¾ cup all-purpose flour
- 1½ teaspoons baking powder
- 1 teaspoon salt
- Blueberries (optional)

1. Combine buttermilk, eggs, sugar and butter in large bowl; beat until well blended. Combine cornmeal, flour, baking powder and salt in medium bowl; stir into buttermilk mixture. Let stand 5 minutes.

2. Lightly grease griddle or large skillet; place over medium heat. Pour about ⅓ cup batter onto hot griddle for each pancake. Cook about 3 minutes or until tops of pancakes are bubbly and appear dry; turn and cook about 2 minutes or until bottoms are golden. Serve with blueberries, if desired.

Makes 4 servings

tip | If your family has a favorite pancake or waffle recipe, make up a homemade "mix." Combine dry ingredients, such as flour, baking powder, sugar and salt in a lidded container. Double or triple the recipe. When you're ready to make breakfast you only need to add eggs and milk. Homemade mix is free from any preservatives and a lot less expensive than the convenience mixes you can buy at the supermarket. Don't forget to shake the mix each time before using.

Banana-Nut Buttermilk Waffles

½ cup walnuts or pecans
2 cups all-purpose flour
¼ cup sugar
2 teaspoons baking powder
1 teaspoon salt
2 eggs, separated
2 cups buttermilk
2 very ripe bananas, mashed (about 1 cup)
¼ cup (½ stick) butter, melted
½ teaspoon vanilla
Syrup and banana slices (optional)
Additional walnuts (optional)

1. Toast walnuts in medium nonstick skillet over medium heat 5 to 8 minutes until fragrant, stirring frequently. Transfer to plate to cool; chop and set aside.

2. Preheat waffle iron according to manufacturer's directions.

3. Meanwhile, combine flour, sugar, baking powder and salt in large bowl. Beat egg yolks in medium bowl. Add buttermilk, mashed bananas, butter, vanilla and walnuts; mix well. Stir buttermilk mixture into flour mixture just until moistened.

4. Beat egg whites in medium bowl with electric mixer at high speed until stiff but not dry. Fold egg whites into batter.

5. Pour ¾ cup batter into waffle iron; cook 4 to 6 minutes or until golden. Serve with syrup, banana slices and additional walnuts, if desired.

Makes 4 servings

Pumpkin Pancakes

- 1 cup all-purpose flour
- 3 tablespoons sugar
- 1 teaspoon baking powder
- ½ teaspoon pumpkin pie spice
- ¼ teaspoon baking soda
- ¼ teaspoon salt
- ¾ cup buttermilk
- ½ cup canned solid-pack pumpkin
- 1 egg
- 1 tablespoon canola oil
- ½ teaspoon vanilla
- Pancake syrup

1. Combine flour, sugar, baking powder, pumpkin pie spice, baking soda and salt in medium bowl; mix well.

2. Whisk together buttermilk, pumpkin, egg, oil and vanilla in small bowl. Add buttermilk mixture to flour mixture; stir just until moistened.

3. Spray griddle or large nonstick skillet with nonstick cooking spray; heat over medium-high heat. Spoon 2 tablespoons batter onto griddle for each pancake; spread batter into 3-inch circle. Cook 2 to 3 minutes or until bubbles form on surface. Turn and cook about 1 minute more or until bottoms are lightly browned. Serve with syrup.

Makes 4 servings

Pumpkin-Cranberry Pancakes: Add ½ cup chopped fresh or frozen (unthawed) cranberries to batter.

Pancakes & Waffles 23

Economical Eggs

Stuffed Picante Muffins

99¢ or LESS

4 eggs
2 tablespoons milk
Nonstick cooking spray
½ cup chopped ham *or* 3 slices Canadian bacon, chopped (3 ounces)
4 English muffin halves, lightly toasted
½ cup (2 ounces) shredded Cheddar cheese
¼ cup picante sauce

1. Combine eggs and milk in medium bowl; whisk until well blended.

2. Coat nonstick skillet with cooking spray; heat over medium heat. Add egg mixture; sprinkle evenly with ham. Cook 2 minutes. When eggs are set around edge, stir until eggs are fluffy and firm.

3. Remove from heat; spoon equal amounts of egg mixture on top of each muffin half. Sprinkle each with 2 tablespoons cheese and top with 1 tablespoon picante sauce. *Makes 4 servings*

Aunt Marilyn's Cinnamon French Toast Casserole

- 1 large loaf French bread, cut into 1½-inch slices
- 3½ cups milk
- 9 eggs
- 1½ cups granulated sugar, divided
- 1 tablespoon vanilla
- ½ teaspoon salt
- 6 to 8 medium baking apples, such as McIntosh or Cortland, peeled and sliced
- 1 teaspoon ground cinnamon
- ½ teaspoon ground nutmeg
- Powdered sugar (optional)

1. Place bread slices in greased 13×9-inch glass baking dish or casserole.

2. Whisk milk, eggs, 1 cup granulated sugar, vanilla and salt in large bowl until well blended. Pour half of mixture over bread. Layer apple slices over bread. Pour remaining half of egg mixture over apples.

3. Combine remaining ½ cup granulated sugar, cinnamon and nutmeg in small bowl; sprinkle over casserole. Cover and refrigerate overnight.

4. Preheat oven to 350°F. Bake, uncovered, 1 hour or until eggs are set. Sprinkle with powdered sugar, if desired.

Makes 6 to 8 servings

Economical Eggs 27

Spinach Sensation

99¢ or Less

- ½ pound bacon slices
- 1 cup (8 ounces) sour cream
- 3 eggs, separated
- 2 tablespoons all-purpose flour
- ⅛ teaspoon black pepper
- 1 package (10 ounces) frozen chopped spinach, thawed and squeezed dry
- ½ cup (2 ounces) shredded sharp Cheddar cheese
- ½ cup dry bread crumbs
- 1 tablespoon butter, melted

1. Preheat oven to 350°F. Spray 2-quart baking dish with nonstick cooking spray.

2. Place bacon in single layer in large skillet; cook over medium heat until crisp. Drain on paper towels. Crumble and set aside.

3. Combine sour cream, egg yolks, flour and pepper in large bowl. Beat egg whites in medium bowl with electric mixer at high speed until stiff peaks form. Gradually fold egg whites into sour cream mixture.

4. Arrange half of spinach in prepared dish. Top with half of sour cream mixture. Sprinkle ¼ cup cheese over sour cream mixture. Sprinkle bacon over cheese. Repeat layers, ending with remaining ¼ cup cheese.

5. Combine bread crumbs and butter in small bowl; sprinkle evenly over cheese. Bake, uncovered, 30 to 35 minutes or until egg mixture is set. Let stand 5 minutes before serving.

Makes 6 servings

Chile Cheese Puff

¾ cup all-purpose flour
1½ teaspoons baking powder
9 eggs
4 cups (16 ounces) shredded Monterey Jack cheese
2 cups (16 ounces) cottage cheese
2 cans (4 ounces each) diced green chiles, drained
1½ teaspoons sugar
¼ teaspoon salt
⅛ teaspoon hot pepper sauce
1 cup salsa

1. Preheat oven to 350°F. Spray 13×9-inch baking dish with nonstick cooking spray.

2. Combine flour and baking powder in small bowl.

3. Whisk eggs in large bowl until blended; stir in Monterey Jack cheese, cottage cheese, chiles, sugar, salt and hot pepper sauce. Add flour mixture; stir just until blended. Pour into prepared dish.

4. Bake, uncovered, 45 minutes or until set. Let stand 5 minutes before serving. Serve with salsa. *Makes 8 servings*

tip Eggs are an eggs-cellent, egg-onomical source of protein. Always store eggs in the original carton in the coldest part of the refrigerator. The carton protects them from picking up odors. Storing eggs in the holders in some refrigerator doors is not recommended. The temperature there is warmer and fluctuates every time the door is opened.

Economical Eggs 31

Crustless Ham & Spinach Tart

99¢ or LESS

- 1 teaspoon olive oil
- 1 cup finely chopped onion
- 2 garlic cloves, minced
- 1 package (10 ounces) frozen chopped spinach, thawed and squeezed dry
- 3 slices deli ham, cut into strips (3 ounces total)
- 1¼ cups milk
- 3 eggs
- 1½ tablespoons all-purpose flour
- 2 teaspoons dried basil
- ½ teaspoon black pepper
- ⅛ teaspoon ground nutmeg
- 6 tablespoons grated Parmesan cheese

1. Preheat oven to 350°F. Lightly spray 9-inch glass pie plate with nonstick cooking spray.

2. Heat oil in medium nonstick skillet over medium-high heat. Add onion and cook 2 minutes or until soft, stirring occasionally. Add garlic and cook 1 minute. Stir in spinach and ham, mixing well. Spread mixture evenly in prepared pie plate.

3. Combine milk, eggs, flour, basil, pepper and nutmeg in medium bowl. Pour over spinach mixture. Bake 50 minutes or until knife inserted into center comes out clean. Sprinkle with cheese.

Makes 6 servings

Economical Eggs 33

Chile-Corn Quiche

1 unbaked 9-inch deep-dish pie crust
1 can (about 8 ounces) whole kernel corn, drained,
1 can (4 ounces) diced mild green chiles, drained
¼ cup thinly sliced green onions
1 cup (4 ounces) shredded Monterey Jack cheese
3 eggs
1½ cups half-and-half
½ teaspoon salt
½ teaspoon ground cumin

1. Preheat oven to 450°F. Line pie crust with foil; partially fill with uncooked beans or rice to weight crust. Bake 10 minutes. Remove foil and beans; continue baking pie crust 5 minutes or until lightly browned. Let cool. *Reduce oven temperature to 375°F.*

2. Combine corn, chiles and green onions in small bowl. Spoon into pie crust; top with cheese. Whisk eggs, half-and-half, salt and cumin in medium bowl. Pour over cheese.

3. Bake 35 to 45 minutes or until filling is puffed and knife inserted into center comes out clean. Let stand 10 minutes before serving.

Makes 6 servings

Canned vegetables, such as the corn and chiles in this recipe, are economical and convenient. They are also usually just as nutritious as fresh ingredients. Because they are generally picked and preserved when ripe, canned vegetables retain most of their nutrients. Fresh produce often sits in warehouses or in transit for weeks before it appears in local markets.

Swiss, Canadian Bacon & Eggs

99¢ or LESS

8 eggs
¼ cup milk
½ teaspoon salt
¼ teaspoon black pepper
¼ cup finely chopped green onions, divided
Nonstick cooking spray
4 slices Canadian bacon, cut in half
1 cup (4 ounces) shredded Monterey Jack or Swiss cheese

1. Preheat broiler.

2. Whisk together eggs, milk, salt and pepper in medium bowl until well blended. Reserve 2 tablespoons green onions; stir remaining green onions into egg mixture.

3. Spray 12-inch ovenproof skillet with cooking spray; heat over medium-low heat. Add egg mixture. Cover and cook 14 minutes or until almost set.

4. Arrange bacon in pinwheel on top of egg mixture. Sprinkle with cheese; broil 2 minutes or until cheese is bubbly. Top with reserved 2 tablespoons green onions. Cut into wedges. Serve immediately.

Makes 4 to 5 servings

Cornmeal, Sausage & Chile Casserole

99¢ or less

- 4 ounces bulk breakfast sausage
- ½ cup diced onion
- ½ medium red bell pepper, diced
- 1 teaspoon ground cumin
- ½ to 1 teaspoon chili powder
- 1 cup reduced-sodium chicken broth
- ½ cup yellow cornmeal
- 3 egg whites
- 1 can (about 4 ounces) diced mild green chiles, drained
- ½ cup (2 ounces) shredded Cheddar cheese
- 3 eggs, beaten
- Salsa (optional)

1. Heat large nonstick skillet over medium-high heat; add sausage, onion and bell pepper. Cook 5 minutes, stirring to break up meat, until sausage is no longer pink and vegetables are crisp-tender. Add cumin and chili powder; cook and stir 1 minute.

2. Add broth to skillet; bring to a boil. Gradually add cornmeal; cook 1 minute, stirring constantly. Transfer mixture to large bowl; cool slightly.

3. Preheat oven to 375°F. Spray 11×7-inch glass baking dish with nonstick cooking spray.

4. Meanwhile, beat egg whites in small bowl with electric mixer at high speed until stiff peaks form. Stir chiles and cheese into cornmeal mixture. Stir in whole eggs. Gently fold beaten egg whites into cornmeal mixture. Spoon mixture into prepared dish.

5. Bake 30 minutes or until center is set and edges are lightly browned. Cool slightly. Serve immediately with salsa, if desired.

Makes 6 servings

Sunny Day Breakfast Burritos

- 1 tablespoon butter
- ½ cup red or green bell pepper, chopped
- 2 green onions, sliced
- 6 eggs
- 2 tablespoons milk
- ¼ teaspoon salt
- 4 (7-inch) flour tortillas, warmed
- ½ cup (2 ounces) shredded Colby jack or Mexican cheese blend
- ½ cup salsa

1. Melt butter in medium skillet over medium heat. Add bell pepper and green onions; cook and stir about 3 minutes or until tender.

2. Beat eggs, milk and salt in medium bowl. Add egg mixture to skillet; reduce heat to low. Cook, stirring gently, until eggs are just set. (Eggs should be soft with no liquid remaining.)

3. Spoon one fourth of egg mixture down center of each tortilla; top with 2 tablespoons cheese. Fold in sides of tortillas to enclose filling. Serve with salsa.

Makes 4 servings

tip | Burritos are a wonderful addition to any cost-conscious kitchen. Fill them with eggs for breakfast or try an endless assortment of other fillings. Use beans, corn or rice to stretch a small amount of leftover beef or pork for a tasty meal the whole family will love.

Muffins & More

Bacon-Cheddar Muffins

2 cups all-purpose flour
¾ cup sugar
2 teaspoons baking powder
½ teaspoon baking soda
½ teaspoon salt
¾ cup plus 2 tablespoons milk
⅓ cup butter, melted and cooled
1 egg
1 cup (4 ounces) shredded Cheddar cheese
6 slices bacon, crisp-cooked and crumbled

1. Preheat oven to 350°F. Grease 12 standard (2½-inch) muffin cups.

2. Combine flour, sugar, baking powder, baking soda and salt in medium bowl. Combine milk, butter and egg in small bowl; mix well. Add milk mixture to flour mixture; stir until blended. Gently stir in cheese and bacon. Spoon batter into prepared muffin cups, filling three-fourths full.

3. Bake 15 to 20 minutes or until toothpick inserted into centers comes out clean. Cool in pan 2 minutes; remove to wire rack. Serve warm or at room temperature. *Makes 6 servings (2 muffins each)*

Raspberry Corn Muffins

1 cup all-purpose flour
¾ cup cornmeal
2 teaspoons baking powder
½ teaspoon baking soda
¼ teaspoon salt
1 cup sour cream
⅓ cup unsweetened apple juice concentrate
1 egg, beaten
1½ cups fresh or frozen raspberries
⅔ cup whipped cream cheese
2 tablespoons raspberry fruit spread

1. Preheat oven to 350°F. Spray 12 standard (2½-inch) muffin cups with nonstick cooking spray.

2. Combine flour, cornmeal, baking powder, baking soda and salt in small bowl. Whisk together sour cream, apple juice concentrate and egg. Add flour mixture to egg mixture. Stir just until dry ingredients are moistened. Gently stir in raspberries. Spoon batter into prepared muffin cups, filling three-fourths full.

3. Bake 18 to 20 minutes or until golden brown. Cool in pan on wire rack 5 minutes. Remove from pan; cool slightly.

4. Combine cream cheese and fruit spread in small serving bowl. Serve with warm muffins.   *Makes 6 servings (2 muffins each)*

Broccoli & Cheddar Scones

99¢ or LESS

2½ cups all-purpose flour
1 tablespoon baking powder
1 tablespoon sugar
2 teaspoons salt
½ teaspoon red pepper flakes
1 cup broccoli florets
½ cup (1 stick) cold butter, cut into pieces
1½ cups (6 ounces) shredded Cheddar cheese
1 cup milk

1. Preheat oven to 400°F. Line baking sheets with parchment paper.

2. Place flour, baking powder, sugar, salt and red pepper flakes in food processor. Process 10 seconds. Add broccoli and butter; process until mixture forms coarse meal, scraping down sides once.

3. Place mixture in large bowl. Add cheese and milk; stir until combined. Transfer dough to floured surface. Knead lightly; divide in half.

4. Press one dough half into 8-inch circle. Cut into 8 wedges; place on baking sheet. Repeat with second half of dough.

5. Bake 15 to 20 minutes or until lightly browned. Serve warm.

Makes 4 servings (4 scones each)

tip Making your own scones is easy and a lot more economical that buying them at a coffee shop or grocery store. Because scones stale quickly, some store-bought versions include stabilizers or preservatives to improve shelf life. Scones are best still warm from the oven—another advantage to baking them at home.

Muffins & More 47

Jumbo Streusel-Topped Raspberry Muffins

2¼ cups all-purpose flour, divided
¼ cup packed brown sugar
2 tablespoons cold butter
¾ cup granulated sugar
2 teaspoons baking powder
½ teaspoon baking soda
½ teaspoon salt
½ teaspoon grated lemon peel
¾ cup plus 2 tablespoons milk
⅓ cup butter, melted
1 egg, beaten
2 cups fresh or frozen raspberries (do not thaw)

1. Preheat oven to 350°F. Grease 6 jumbo (3½-inch) muffin cups.

2. For topping, combine ¼ cup flour and brown sugar in small bowl. Cut in cold butter with pastry blender or two knives until mixture forms coarse crumbs.

3. Reserve ¼ cup flour in medium bowl. Combine remaining 1¾ cups flour, sugar, baking powder, baking soda, salt and lemon peel in medium bowl. Combine milk, melted butter and egg in small bowl.

4. Add milk mixture to flour mixture; stir until almost blended. Toss raspberries with reserved flour just until coated; gently fold raspberries into muffin batter. Spoon batter into prepared muffin cups, filling three-fourths full. Sprinkle with topping.

5. Bake 25 to 30 minutes or until toothpick inserted into centers comes out clean. Cool in pan 2 minutes; remove to wire rack. Serve warm or at room temperature. *Makes 6 servings*

Variation: For smaller muffins, spoon batter into 12 standard (2½-inch) greased or paper-lined muffin cups. Bake at 350°F 20 to 24 minutes or until toothpick inserted into centers comes out clean. Makes 12 muffins.

Cranberry Coffee Cake

½ cup walnuts or pecans, coarsely chopped and toasted
¾ cup sugar, divided
1 cup plus 1 tablespoon all-purpose flour, divided
½ cup (1 stick) plus 1 tablespoon butter, softened, divided
½ teaspoon ground cinnamon
½ teaspoon baking soda
½ teaspoon baking powder
½ teaspoon salt
1 egg
2 to 3 teaspoons grated orange peel
½ teaspoon vanilla
½ cup sour cream
⅔ cup dried cranberries

1. Preheat oven to 350°F. Grease and flour 8-inch square baking dish.

2. For topping, combine walnuts, ¼ cup sugar, 1 tablespoon flour, 1 tablespoon butter and cinnamon in small bowl; rub mixture with fingertips until blended.

3. Sift remaining 1 cup flour, baking soda, baking powder and salt into medium bowl. Beat remaining ½ cup sugar and ½ cup butter in large bowl with electric mixer at medium-high speed 2 to 3 minutes or until light and fluffy. Add egg, orange peel and vanilla; mix well.

4. Alternately add flour mixture and sour cream to sugar mixture; beat at low speed until blended. *Do not overmix.* Fold in cranberries. Spread batter in prepared pan; sprinkle with topping.

5. Bake 25 to 30 minutes or until toothpick inserted into center comes out clean. Cool 5 minutes before cutting.

Makes 6 to 8 servings

Carrot & Oat Muffins

½ cup milk
½ cup unsweetened applesauce
2 eggs, beaten
1 tablespoon canola oil
½ cup shredded carrot (1 large carrot)
1 cup minus 2 tablespoons old-fashioned oats
¾ cup whole wheat flour
¾ cup all-purpose flour
⅓ cup sugar
1 teaspoon ground cinnamon
1½ teaspoons baking powder
½ teaspoon baking soda
¼ teaspoon salt
¼ cup finely chopped walnuts (optional)

1. Preheat oven to 350°F. Spray 12 standard (2½-inch) muffin cups with nonstick cooking spray.

2. Beat milk, applesauce, eggs and oil in large bowl until blended. Stir in carrot. Combine oats, whole wheat flour, all-purpose flour, sugar, cinnamon, baking powder, baking soda and salt in separate bowl. Add flour mixture to applesauce mixture. Stir just until batter is moistened.

3. Spoon batter into prepared muffin cups, filling two-thirds full. Sprinkle 1 teaspoon walnuts over each muffin, if desired. Bake 20 to 22 minutes or until muffins are golden brown. Cool in pan 5 minutes; remove to wire rack.

Makes 4 servings (3 muffins each)

Muffins & More 53

Morning Muffins with Blueberries

99¢ OR LESS

½ cup plus 1 tablespoon sugar, divided
⅛ teaspoon ground cinnamon
1¾ cups all-purpose flour
2 teaspoons baking powder
½ teaspoon salt
½ cup milk
¼ cup vegetable oil
1 egg
1 teaspoon vanilla
1 teaspoon grated orange peel
1 cup fresh or frozen blueberries

1. Preheat oven to 400°F. Grease 12 standard (2½-inch) muffin cups or line with paper baking cups. Combine 1 tablespoon sugar and cinnamon in small bowl; set aside.

2. Combine flour, remaining ½ cup sugar, baking powder and salt in large bowl. Beat milk, oil, egg, vanilla and orange peel in small bowl until blended. Make a well in center of flour mixture; stir in milk mixture just until moistened. Fold in blueberries. Spoon evenly into prepared muffin cups, filling about two-thirds full.

3. Bake 15 to 18 minutes or until toothpick inserted into centers comes out clean. Immediately sprinkle sugar mixture over hot muffins. Remove to wire racks. Serve warm.

Makes 4 servings (3 muffins each)

Tip: For muffins with larger tops, fill the muffin cups almost full and bake as directed. The recipe will make about 8 big-top muffins.

Apple Ring Coffeecake

3 cups all-purpose flour
1 teaspoon baking soda
1 teaspoon salt
1 teaspoon ground cinnamon
1 cup walnuts, chopped
1½ cups granulated sugar
1 cup vegetable oil
2 eggs
2 teaspoons vanilla
2 medium tart apples, peeled, cored and chopped
Powdered sugar (optional)

1. Preheat oven to 325°F. Grease 10-inch tube pan.

2. Sift flour, baking soda, salt and cinnamon into large bowl. Stir in walnuts.

3. Combine granulated sugar, oil, eggs and vanilla in medium bowl. Stir in apples. Stir into flour mixture just until moistened.

4. Spoon batter into prepared pan, spreading evenly. Bake 1 hour or until toothpick inserted near center comes out clean. Cool in pan on wire rack 10 minutes. Run knife around edge to loosen cake; remove from pan. Cool completely on wire rack.

5. Transfer to serving plate. Sprinkle with powdered sugar; serve immediately. Store leftover cake in airtight container.

Makes 12 servings

Double Chocolate Zucchini Muffins

99¢ or LESS

2⅓ cups all-purpose flour
1¼ cups sugar
⅓ cup unsweetened cocoa powder
2 teaspoons baking powder
1½ teaspoons ground cinnamon
1 teaspoon baking soda
½ teaspoon salt
1 cup sour cream
½ cup vegetable oil
2 eggs, beaten
¼ cup milk
1 cup milk chocolate chips
1 cup shredded zucchini

1. Preheat oven to 400°F. Line 12 jumbo (3½-inch) muffin cups with paper baking cups or spray with nonstick cooking spray.

2. Combine flour, sugar, cocoa, baking powder, cinnamon, baking soda and salt in large bowl. Blend sour cream, oil, eggs and milk in medium bowl. Stir into flour mixture just until moistened. Fold in chocolate chips and zucchini. Spoon batter into prepared muffin cups, filling half full.

3. Bake 25 to 30 minutes or until toothpick inserted into centers comes out clean. Cool in pan on wire rack 5 minutes. Remove to wire rack to cool. Store tightly covered at room temperature.

Makes 12 servings

Variation: For standard-size muffins, spoon batter into 18 standard (2½-inch) paper-lined or greased muffin cups. Bake 18 to 20 minutes or until toothpick inserted into centers comes out clean. Makes 18 muffins.

English-Style Scones

3 eggs
½ cup whipping cream
1½ teaspoons vanilla
2 cups all-purpose flour
2 teaspoons baking powder
¼ teaspoon salt
¼ cup (½ stick) cold butter
¼ cup finely chopped pitted dates
¼ cup golden raisins or currants
1 teaspoon water
Orange marmalade (optional)
Whipped cream or butter (optional)

1. Preheat oven to 375°F. Lightly grease large baking sheet.

2. Beat 2 eggs, cream and vanilla in medium bowl. Combine flour, baking powder and salt in medium bowl. Cut in butter with pastry blender or two knives until mixture resembles coarse crumbs. Stir in dates and raisins. Add cream mixture; mix just until dry ingredients are moistened.

3. With floured hands, knead dough four times on lightly floured surface. Place dough on prepared baking sheet; pat into 8-inch circle. With sharp wet knife, gently score dough into six wedges, cutting three-fourths of the way through dough. Beat remaining egg with water; brush lightly over dough.

4. Bake 18 to 20 minutes or until golden brown. Cool 5 minutes on wire rack. Cut into wedges. Serve warm with marmalade and whipped cream, if desired. *Makes 6 scones*

Hot & Hearty

Sausage-Topped Cornbread

- ¾ pound bulk sausage
- 1 onion, chopped
- ½ red bell pepper, chopped
- 1 jalapeño pepper,* chopped
- 1½ cups (6 ounces) shredded Cheddar cheese
- 1 package (8½ ounces) cornbread mix, plus ingredients to prepare mix

*Jalapeño peppers can sting and irritate the skin, so wear rubber gloves when handling peppers and do not touch eyes.

1. Preheat oven to 400°F. Generously spray 9-inch round cake pan with nonstick cooking spray.

2. Cook sausage, onion, bell pepper and jalapeño pepper in large skillet over medium-high heat 6 to 8 minutes, stirring to break up meat. Spread sausage mixture evenly in prepared pan. Sprinkle with cheese.

3. Prepare cornbread mix according to package directions; pour over cheese. Bake 20 to 25 minutes or until golden brown. Cool 5 minutes in pan. Invert onto plate. Serve immediately. *Makes 8 servings*

tip | Sausage is available in endless variety. Choose your family's favorite or the one at the best price. If bulk sausage is unavailable, substitute sausage links and simply remove the meat from the casing before cooking.

Mixed Berry Whole Grain Coffee Cake

99¢ or LESS

- 1¼ cups all-purpose flour, divided
- ¾ cup quick oats
- ¾ cup packed light brown sugar
- 3 tablespoons butter
- 1 cup whole wheat flour
- 1 cup milk
- ¾ cup granulated sugar
- ¼ cup canola oil
- 1 egg, slightly beaten
- 1 tablespoon baking powder
- 1 teaspoon ground cinnamon
- ½ teaspoon salt
- 1½ cups frozen unsweetened mixed berries, thawed and drained *or* 2 cups fresh berries
- ¼ cup chopped walnuts

1. Preheat oven to 350°F. Spray 9×5-inch loaf pan with nonstick cooking spray.

2. Combine ¼ cup all-purpose flour, oats, brown sugar and butter in small bowl. Rub with fingers until crumbly; set aside.

3. Combine remaining 1 cup all-purpose flour, whole wheat flour, milk, granulated sugar, oil, egg, baking powder, cinnamon and salt in large bowl. Beat 1 to 2 minutes until well blended. Fold in berries.

4. Spread batter in prepared pan. Sprinkle evenly with reserved oat mixture. Top with walnuts. Bake 38 to 40 minutes or until toothpick inserted into center comes out clean. Serve warm.

Makes 8 servings

Biscuit & Sausage Bake

- 2 cups biscuit baking mix
- ½ cup milk
- 1 egg
- 1 teaspoon vanilla
- 1 cup fresh or frozen blueberries
- 6 fully cooked breakfast sausage links, thawed if frozen
- Pancake syrup (optional)

1. Preheat oven to 350°F. Spray 8-inch square baking pan with nonstick cooking spray.

2. Stir baking mix, milk, egg and vanilla in medium bowl. Gently fold in blueberries. (Batter will be stiff.) Spread batter in prepared pan.

3. Cut each sausage link into small pieces; sprinkle over batter.

4. Bake 22 minutes or until top is lightly browned. Cut into squares; serve with syrup, if desired. *Makes 6 servings*

tip Blueberries freeze quite well. Next time they are in season, stock up and freeze your own to preserve the wonderful flavor and health benefits blueberries offer. To freeze, arrange the blueberries in a single layer in a baking pan. Freeze until they are solid and then transfer the blueberries to a resealable freezer bag. You'll be able to easily remove the quantity you want and return the rest to the freezer.

Breakfast Pizza

- 2 cups refrigerated or frozen shredded hash brown potatoes, thawed
- ½ cup finely chopped onion
- Nonstick cooking spray
- ¼ cup tomato paste
- 2 tablespoons water
- ½ teaspoon dried oregano
- 2 eggs, lightly beaten
- ½ cup (2 ounces) shredded mozzarella cheese
- 2 tablespoons imitation bacon bits

1. Combine potatoes and onion in small bowl.

2. Lightly spray medium nonstick skillet with cooking spray. Add potato mixture; flatten with spatula. Cook 7 to 9 minutes per side or until both sides are lightly browned.

3. Mix tomato paste and water in small bowl; spread evenly over potatoes in skillet. Sprinkle oregano over tomato mixture. Pour eggs over potato mixture.

4. Cover and cook 4 minutes. Sprinkle mozzarella and bacon bits over eggs. Cover and cook 1 minute.

5. Slide pizza from skillet onto serving plate. Cut into 4 wedges.

Makes 2 to 4 servings

 One small onion should yield about ½ cup chopped. If you ever end up with more chopped onion than a recipe calls for, freeze the extra for another time. You'll have a head start on another recipe and won't waste food.

Cheddary Sausage Frittata

4 eggs
¼ cup milk
1 package (about 7 ounces) breakfast sausage patties
1 poblano pepper,* seeded and chopped
1 cup (4 ounces) shredded Cheddar cheese

*Poblano peppers are dark green chiles about 4 inches long. They can be found in Mexican markets and many supermarkets. They can be mild to slightly hot. A green bell pepper may be substituted.

1. Preheat broiler. Combine eggs and milk in medium bowl; whisk until well blended. Set aside.

2. Heat 12-inch ovenproof nonstick skillet over medium-high heat. Add sausage; cook and stir 4 minutes or until no longer pink, stirring to break up meat. Drain fat.

3. Add pepper to skillet; cook and stir 2 minutes or until crisp-tender. Add egg mixture; stir until blended. Cover; cook over medium-low heat 10 minutes or until eggs are almost set.

4. Sprinkle cheese over frittata; broil 2 minutes or until cheese is melted. Cut into 4 wedges. Serve immediately.   *Makes 4 servings*

Tip: If skillet is not ovenproof, wrap handle in heavy-duty aluminum foil before broiling.

Individual Spinach & Bacon Quiches

99¢ or LESS

3 slices bacon
½ small onion, chopped
1 package (10 ounces) frozen chopped spinach, thawed and squeezed dry
½ teaspoon black pepper
⅛ teaspoon ground nutmeg
Pinch salt
1 container (15 ounces) whole milk ricotta cheese
2 cups (8 ounces) shredded mozzarella cheese
1 cup grated Parmesan cheese
3 eggs, lightly beaten

1. Preheat oven to 350°F. Spray 10 standard (2½-inch) muffin cups with nonstick cooking spray.

2. Cook bacon in large skillet over medium-high heat until crisp. Transfer to paper towels. Let cool; crumble.

3. Cook and stir onion in same skillet 5 minutes or until tender. Add spinach, pepper, nutmeg and salt. Cook and stir over medium heat about 3 minutes or until liquid evaporates. Remove from heat. Stir in bacon; cool.

4. Combine cheeses in large bowl. Add eggs; stir until well blended. Add cooled spinach mixture; mix well.

5. Divide mixture evenly among prepared muffin cups. Bake 40 minutes or until filling is set. Let stand 10 minutes. Run knife around edges to release. Serve hot or refrigerate and serve cold.

Makes 10 servings

Bratwurst Skillet Breakfast

99¢ or LESS

- 1½ pounds red potatoes
- 3 bratwurst links (about ¾ pound)
- 2 tablespoons butter
- 1½ teaspoons caraway seeds (optional)
- 4 cups shredded red cabbage
- Salt and black pepper

1. Cut potatoes into ½-inch pieces. Place in microwavable baking dish. Cover; microwave on HIGH 3 minutes; stir. Microwave 2 minutes more or until just tender; set aside.

2. Meanwhile, cut sausage into ¼-inch slices. Cook sausage in large skillet over medium-high heat 8 minutes or until browned and cooked through. Transfer to paper towels. Drain fat.

3. Melt butter in same skillet. Add potatoes and caraway seeds, if desired. Cook, stirring occasionally, 6 to 8 minutes or until potatoes are golden and tender. Return sausage to skillet; stir in cabbage. Cover and cook 3 minutes or until cabbage is slightly wilted. Uncover; cook and stir 3 to 4 minutes more or until cabbage is just tender.

Makes 4 servings

Hot & Hearty 75

Mushroom & Onion Egg Bake

1 tablespoon vegetable oil
1 can (4 ounces) sliced mushrooms, drained
4 green onions, chopped
1 cup cottage cheese
6 eggs
1 cup sour cream
2 tablespoons all-purpose flour
¼ teaspoon salt
⅛ teaspoon black pepper
Dash hot pepper sauce

1. Preheat oven to 350°F. Grease shallow 1-quart baking dish.

2. Heat oil in medium skillet over medium heat. Add mushrooms and onions; cook until tender.

3. Blend cottage cheese in blender or food processor until almost smooth. Add eggs, sour cream, flour, salt, black pepper and hot pepper sauce; blend until combined. Stir in mushrooms and onions.

4. Pour into prepared baking dish. Bake about 40 minutes or until knife inserted near center comes out clean. *Makes 6 servings*

tip | Try serving breakfast for dinner! Main course dishes, such as omelets, pancakes and this Mushroom & Onion Egg Bake, make filling, economical family meals. Even confirmed carnivores can go vegetarian one night a week. Chances are your family won't even notice the missing meat, but your budget will.

Ham & Egg Enchiladas

BUDGET FRIENDLY

- 2 tablespoons butter
- 3 green onions, sliced
- ½ cup diced ham
- 8 eggs
- 8 (7- to 8-inch) flour tortillas
- ½ cup (2 ounces) shredded pepper jack cheese
- 1 can (10 ounces) enchilada sauce
- ½ cup salsa
- **Additional shredded pepper jack cheese (optional)**

1. Preheat oven to 350°F.

2. Melt butter in large nonstick skillet over medium heat. Add onions; cook and stir 1 minute. Add ham; cook and stir 1 minute.

3. Lightly beat eggs in medium bowl with whisk. Add to skillet; cook until eggs are set but still soft, stirring occasionally.

4. Spoon about ⅓ cup egg mixture evenly down center of each tortilla; top with 1 tablespoon cheese. Roll up tortillas and place seam side down in shallow 11×7-inch baking dish.

5. Combine enchilada sauce and salsa in small bowl; pour evenly over enchiladas.

6. Cover dish with foil; bake 20 minutes. Uncover; sprinkle with additional cheese, if desired. Continue baking 10 minutes or until enchiladas are heated through and cheese is melted. Serve immediately.

Makes 4 to 5 servings

A
Apple Ring Coffeecake, 56
Aunt Marilyn's Cinnamon French Toast Casserole, 26

B
Bacon-Cheddar Muffins, 42
Banana-Nut Buttermilk Waffles, 20
Biscuit & Sausage Bake, 66
Blueberry Pancakes with Blueberry-Spice Syrup, 16
Blueberry-Spice Syrup, 16
Bratwurst Skillet Breakfast, 74
Breakfast Pizza, 68
Broccoli & Cheddar Scones, 46

C
Carrot & Oat Muffins, 52
Cheddary Sausage Frittata, 70
Chile Cheese Puff, 30
Chile-Corn Quiche, 34
Chocolate Cherry Pancakes, 6
Classic Waffles, 12
Cornmeal Pancakes, 18
Cornmeal, Sausage & Chile Casserole, 38
Cranberry Coffee Cake, 50
Crustless Ham & Spinach Tart, 32

D
Devil's Food Pancakes, 9
Double Chocolate Zucchini Muffins, 58

E
English-Style Scones, 60

H
Ham & Egg Enchiladas, 78

I
Individual Spinach & Bacon Quiches, 72

J
Jumbo Streusel-Topped Raspberry Muffins, 48

M
Mixed Berry Whole Grain Coffeecake, 64
Morning Muffins with Blueberries, 54
Mushroom & Onion Egg Bake, 76

O
Oatmeal Pecan Pancakes, 8

P
Peach Pecan Upside-Down Pancake, 14
Puffy Pancake, 4
Pumpkin Pancakes, 22

R
Raspberry Corn Muffins, 44

S
Sausage-Topped Cornbread, 62
Spinach Sensation, 28
Stuffed Picante Muffins, 24
Sunny Day Breakfast Burritos, 40
Swiss, Canadian Bacon & Eggs, 36